Witness to History

The French Revolution

Sean Connolly

Heinemann
LIBRARY

www.heinemann.co.uk/library
Visit our website to find out more inform

To order:
☎ Phone 44 (0) 1865 888066
🖹 Send a fax to 44 (0) 1865 314091
💻 Visit the Heinemann Bookshop at www.l
catalogue and order online.

First published in Great Britain by Heinemann Library,
Halley Court, Jordan Hill, Oxford
OX2 8EJ, part of Harcourt Education.
Heinemann is a registered trademark of
Harcourt Education Ltd.

© Harcourt Education Ltd 2003
First published in paperback in 2004
The moral right of the proprietor has been asserted.

Editorial: Sarah Eason and Kathy Peltan
Design: Ron Kamen and Celia Floyd
Picture Research: Maria Joannou
Production: Viv Hichens

Originated by Ambassador Litho Ltd
Printed and bound in Hong Kong, China
by South China Printing

ISBN 0 431 17030 4 (hardback)
07 06 05 04 03
10 9 8 7 6 5 4 3 2 1

ISBN 0 431 17036 3 (paperback)
08 07 06 05 04
10 9 8 7 6 5 4 3 2 1

British Library Cataloguing in Publication Data
Connolly, Sean, 1956–
  French Revolution. – (Witness to History)
  1. France – History – Revolution, 1789–1799 – Juvenile
  literature
  I. Title
  944'.04

A full catalogue record for this book is available from the
British Library.

Acknowledgements
The publishers would like to thank the following for
permission to reproduce photographs:
AKG London pp.**28**, **43**; Bridgeman Art Library pp.**4**, **44**,
46, **50**; (Musee de la Ville de Paris) pp.**14**, **18**, **38**, **40**;
(Bibliotheque Nationale) p.**11**; (Fogg Art Museum, Harvard
University Art Museums) p.**22**; (Lauros-Giraudon) pp.**7**, **51**;
(Musee Carnavalet) p.**32**; (Musee de Beaux-Arts, Rouen)
p.**12**; British Library p.**6**; Corbis (Gianni Dagli) p.**30**; Hulton
Getty p.**48**; Mary Evans Picture Library pp. **5**, **13**, **16**, **20**,
24, **26**, **35**, **36**; Robert Harding Picture Library p.**8**; Robert
Harding Picture Library (David Martyn Hughes) p.**10**.

Cover photograph of prisoners being taken to the
guillotine, reproduced with permission of Mary Evans
Picture Library.

The publishers would like to thank Bob Rees, historian and
Assistant Head Teacher, for his assistance in the
preparation of this book.

Words appearing in bold, **like this,** are explained in the Glossary.

Contents

Introduction 4
How do we know? 6
The old system 8
Election fever 10
The National Assembly 12
The Tennis Court Oath 14
The king responds 16
Storming the Bastille 18
Confusion and order 20
The Rights of Man 22
Defining the new country 24
Controlling the king 26
Calls for war 28
The 'September massacres' 30
The king is dead 32
Wars on all fronts 34
The Committee of Public Safety 36
The Reign of Terror 38
The Fall of Robespierre 40
The Directory 42
The rise of Napoleon 44
Transforming the Revolution 46
Legacy of the Revolution 48
What have we learnt from the
    French Revolution? 50
Timeline 52
Find out more 53
List of primary sources 53
Glossary 54
Index 56

Introduction

You can say that the French Revolution changed the course of history. Many of us – without even knowing it – come across it in our everyday lives. We have heard of the **guillotine**, the dreadful machine for beheading people, but we might not know that thousands of French people cheered each time the blade dropped on a victim's neck. We know that 14 July is the French national holiday – but how many of us know that it marks the fall of the hated Bastille prison, where French kings used to lock up their enemies?

The French were not the first people to change the way they were governed. Nearly 100 years before the French Revolution began in 1789, Britain's Glorious Revolution set limits on the king's power in order to protect the public. In 1776, American **colonists** staged a revolution to gain independence from Britain.

Louis XVI ruled France when the French Revolution started. He was beheaded in 1793.

Tied to tradition

Yet the French Revolution had a flavour all of its own – with the people of France rising up to rid the country of an ancient and unjust ruling system. In the late eighteenth century, the country was held back by a system of laws which benefited only a small group of French people. Most French people had very little say in how the country was run, although they paid enormous taxes and worked long hours. By the 1780s, it became clear that the king, along with the nobles and **clergy**, was struggling to make this outdated system work. The French people responded by rushing into a search for a better system of government.

The ordinary people of France worked hard to scrape a poor living. They soon began to realize that the government cared little for their welfare.

No turning back

The fall of the hated Bastille prison in July 1789 was the most visible early sign of the French Revolution. Elected members of the National Assembly in France struggled to write a new **constitution**, in order to put right the wrongs that had triggered unrest. During these years, there was always the danger that the Revolution would be stopped dead in its tracks – either by crowds of people rioting and getting out of control, or by the foreign supporters of King Louis XVI. The French people – and their new rulers – had to face hard choices as the Revolution progressed.

It soon became clear that there was no place for a king in the new-style France of the early 1790s. **Radicals** argued that the gains of the French Revolution would only be kept by executing the king. Louis XVI was beheaded in 1793. Before long, thousands more French men and women would lose their heads. Nonetheless, despite the violence that was an almost constant feature, the Revolution succeeded in building a France that was richer, stronger and fairer.

How do we know?

By studying history, we can learn about the events of the past. If, for example, we need to find out about the fall of the Roman Empire or about the Norman invasion of England, we can find many books, articles and other material about these subjects. They can tell us when and how these events took place, as well as who were the leading characters. They will often explain why things have happened, by giving the background to the events. They will also describe how the events themselves changed the course of history.

These histories are often written many years (sometimes many centuries) after the events they describe. Like any story that is told, some changes can creep into the accounts. Perhaps the historian does not like French people, or Romans, or military leaders generally. Such an attitude of mind can affect how a story is told, because the historian may present the facts as he or she would have liked them to occur. This kind of personal opinion is called **bias**, and can make some historical accounts unreliable.

Of course, a historian might not be biased, but he or she may still rely on other accounts that were also written long after the original events. Such accounts are called **secondary sources**, because the historian arrives at them second-hand. Here again, we must take care in deciding on the truth. The second historian might be repeating the bias or even mistakes of the previous historians.

The Reading Room at the British Museum has one of the world's greatest collections of historical sources.

Getting to the source

This book aims to use **primary sources** to tell the story of the French Revolution. These are the 'first-hand' accounts of events. Many of the leading figures in the French Revolution were excellent writers and left a wide choice of documents which reveal their thoughts at crucial times. Others were skilful **orators**, and sometimes we have been able to find a written record of a speech from that time. However, the thoughts and words of the ordinary French people are hard to find in written form. There are two reasons for this. Firstly, most ordinary people were too poor to have their words published. The second reason is more important: many of the key players – the rioting crowds, the captors of the Bastille (see pages 18–19) or those watching the king lose his head (see pages 32–33) – were unable to read or write.

Making our minds up

Of course, not every primary source is without bias, and that is true of some of the sources you will find in this book. Personal diaries and accounts tell the truth, but only so far as the writer can know it. The letter written by Marie Antoinette (see page 9) and the account of the fall of the Bastille (see page 19) were written by people who could not – or would not – understand the full picture of what was going on around them. Other accounts were meant to urge French people to victory. Danton's stirring call to arms (see page 35) and *The Times* report of the 'September massacres' (see page 31) are examples of such **propaganda**. By recognizing the shortcomings of such primary sources, we can use them wisely to piece together the complicated jigsaw puzzle that is the French Revolution.

Our knowledge of Marie Antoinette, wife of King Louis XVI, comes from a mixture of historical accounts and her own writings.

The old system

At the end of the eighteenth century, France had a system of government that was old-fashioned and, in many ways, deeply unfair. The people were divided into three groups, or 'estates'. The First Estate (the **clergy**) and the Second Estate (the nobles) enjoyed many privileges. Between them, they owned most of the best land in France. The Third Estate (mainly peasants and poor city dwellers, but also what we would now term the 'middle class') was the largest group, but it had the least power. Representatives of these three groups were supposed to meet in the Estates-General, a type of parliament. The system favoured the first two estates, which could vote down almost any proposal made by the Third Estate. Moreover, the king had to summon the Estates-General – and this had not happened since 1614.

King Louis XVI had ruled France since 1774. On coming to the throne, he increased taxes to raise more money. The Third Estate was hit hardest – the king, as usual, did not want to anger the nobles by reducing their income. By the late 1780s, the French people were growing impatient for change. They were also shocked by the way Louis and his wife, Marie Antoinette, spent large sums of money on banquets, balls and entertainment. For their part, the royal couple were unaware of the daily lives of the ordinary people. They believed that the cheers and applause that greeted them were heartfelt.

Large and beautiful chateaux, such as this one at Blois, were owned by members of the First Estate – a small group of privileged people.

Marie Antoinette's letter

In 1770, Marie Antoinette, daughter of Empress Maria Theresa of Austria, became the wife of the **Dauphin**, who was later crowned King Louis XVI. The following extract, taken from a letter to her mother, shows how shielded she was from life in France.

Versailles, 14 June

My dearest mother,—

... On Tuesday I had a **fête** which I shall never forget all my life. We made our entrance into Paris. As for honours, we received all that we could possibly imagine; but they, though very good in their way, were not what touched me most. What was really moving was the tenderness and earnestness of the poor people, who, in spite of the taxes with which they are overwhelmed, were so very happy to see us. When we went to walk in the Tuileries, the crowd was so large that it was three-quarters of an hour before we could move either forward or backward. The dauphin and I gave repeated orders to the Guards not to beat any one, which had a very good effect. Such excellent order was kept during the whole day that, in spite of the enormous crowd which followed us everywhere, not a person was hurt.

When we returned from our walk we went up to an open terrace and stayed there half an hour. I cannot describe to you, my dear mamma, the joy and affection which everyone exhibited towards us. Before we left, we kissed our hands to the people, which gave them great pleasure. What a happy thing indeed it is for persons in our rank to gain the love of a whole nation so cheaply.

Election fever

During his first fourteen years as king, Louis XVI had not been able to improve conditions in France. The country had an enormous debt. Heavy taxes crippled most poor people, and industry lagged behind that of France's old rival, Britain. The new ideas of the period known as the **Enlightenment** were leading to calls for more justice and fairness in everyday life.

In 1788, Louis XVI called for elections to the Estates-General. Unlike today, where nearly all adults are able to vote in most countries, eighteenth-century France had strict limits on who could vote. Only land-owning men had the right to vote, although many of those who did qualify (including doctors, lawyers and other educated men) were in the Third Estate, like the ordinary village and town folk. They welcomed the chance to influence the future of their country, and the election campaigns were lively. The king suspended **censorship** laws, which led to a flow of **pamphlets** calling for all sorts of changes. By the time the Estates-General met in Versailles, a town south of Paris, in May 1789, the representatives of the Third Estate had many firm proposals – and they were in no mood to be ignored.

The magnificent Palace of Versailles was built in the seventeenth century by Louis XIV as the royal residence.

Complaints and suggestions

The following articles are taken from some of the many *cahiers* (French for 'notebook'), which listed the people's complaints and suggestions for improved living conditions. The articles here seem sensible and fair, but in 1789 they were considered **radical**.

Art. 3.   Frenchmen should regard as laws of the kingdom only those which have been prepared by the National Assembly and approved by the king.

Art. 10. Representatives of the Third Estate should behave in the same way as the representatives of the First and Second Estates, when they address the king.

Art. 17. All distinctions in punishments shall be abolished. Crimes committed by citizens of the different Estates shall be punished under the same law and in the same manner.

Art. 21. No tax shall be legal unless accepted by the representatives of the people and sanctioned by the king.

Art. 22. Because all Frenchmen receive the same benefit from the government, and are equally interested in its maintenance, they should be taxed equally.

Art. 46. Members of all Estates should be able to take up any type of work without exception.

Art. 64. Judges of all law courts shall be obliged to keep to the letter of the law, and may never change or interpret the law at their pleasure.

The 1788 elections caused much excitement, and pamphlets calling for change were distributed in towns and villages.

The National Assembly

People of Paris and other French cities were taking a great interest in the growing political activity in France. Booklets and newspapers called for great changes, often demanding a greater say for the Third Estate. Many people believed that the representatives at the Estates-General in Versailles had a duty to bring about these changes.

All through May 1789, and into June, those representatives argued about the number of votes each Estate should have. Those in the First and Second Estates favoured the existing system, which gave an equal number of votes to each Estate, even though **clergy** and nobles made up only a tiny proportion of the country as a whole. The Third Estate (which had the most representatives) preferred a system of majority voting, which would give it the greatest say. Representatives of the first two Estates blocked this idea. Finally, on 17 June, the Third Estate representatives, led by Honoré Gabriel Riqueti, Comte de Mirabeau (a nobleman who had switched sides), took action, and declared itself the National Assembly. The ordinary people had defied those in power – and the king himself.

Arthur Young's account
Arthur Young, an English traveller, was fascinated by the political excitement in Paris at the start of June 1789. On page 13 he describes a visit to the Palais-Royal garden, which had become a centre for political debate and rumour.

When the king's messenger ordered the representatives of the Third Estate to leave, their leader, the Comte de Mirabeau, said, 'Go and tell your master that we are here by the will of the people and we shall not budge save at the point of a bayonet.'

The fashionable Palais-Royal gardens in Paris became a place for speeches and political debate.

I went to the Palais-Royal to see what new things were published, and to obtain a catalogue of all of them. Every hour produces something new. Thirteen publications came out today, sixteen yesterday and ninety-two last week. One can scarcely squeeze from the door to the counter. Nearly all of these publications are in favour of liberty, and are often furious with the clergy and nobles. But the coffee-houses in the Palais-Royal are even more astonishing; they are not only crowded inside, but there are expectant crowds at the doors and windows, listening with open mouths to certain **orators**, who address their audiences from chairs and tables. You can hardly imagine the eagerness with which they are heard, and the thunder of applause they receive for every word they say against the present government.

The Tennis Court Oath

The establishment of the National Assembly by the Third Estate was a serious challenge to the king and to the old system. The National Assembly then took a further step, into an area that really mattered – money. One of its first acts was to pass a new law which gave it, and it alone, the right to decide on taxes. This was a real display of defiance towards the royal government.

After hearing about this, Louis XVI acted quickly. He banned the National Assembly from its meeting hall. But on 20 June 1789, the National Assembly responded by meeting at a Versailles tennis court. In the so-called Tennis Court Oath, its representatives swore that the National Assembly would not **dissolve** until it had drawn up a **constitution** for France. This would guarantee many rights to French people, especially benefiting the Third Estate.

The Third Estate was growing in strength, helped by splits in the ranks of the First and Second Estates. Many lower-ranking **clergy** and a number of **liberal** nobles broke away to join forces with the National Assembly. The king, of course, feared the strength of this united front. His own position would be stronger if the people were divided – that way, they would have less power to go against him. He could see, however, that opposition was gradually mounting against him.

The National Assembly gathered at a tennis court at Versailles, where they vowed to draft a new constitution.

Emmanuel-Joseph Sieyès's argument

Emmanuel-Joseph Sieyès, a priest, could have represented the First Estate but chose to support the cause of the Third Estate. His short work, 'What is the Third Estate?', published in 1789, was central to the thinking that led to the Tennis Court Oath. He argued that the Third Estate was a true reflection of the country as a whole.

The Third Estate is like a strong and robust man who has one arm still tied in chains. If we were to get rid of an unfair system which favours privileged people only, the nation would be nothing less, but something more. Therefore, what is the Third Estate? It is everything; but it is tied in chains and **oppressed**. Nothing can succeed without it. Everything would be infinitely better if it existed alone.

It is not enough to show that privileged people, far from being useful to the nation, are, in fact, bad for it. It is necessary to prove that nobility is not necessary for society. In fact, it may even be a burden on a nation, and it certainly cannot make up a nation all on its own.

What is a nation? A body of people together, living under a common law, and represented by the same legal system. The Third Estate, therefore, embraces everything that belongs to the nation; and everything that is not the Third Estate cannot be regarded as belonging to the nation. What is the Third Estate? It is the whole; it is everything.

The king responds

The setting up of the National Assembly sent shock waves through France. Louis XVI was furious, but he also knew that his position had become weaker, because many members of the royal army supported the new Assembly. It would be impossible to crush the National Assembly without risking outright revolt. However, Louis felt that he had to prove that he still led the country.

On 23 June 1789, he addressed the National Assembly. His main aim was to keep the separate rights of the First, Second and Third Estates. To demonstrate his power, he paid for loyal foreign soldiers to go to Versailles and Paris. He also dismissed the popular (and **liberal**) minister Jacques Necker from the government. However, the Third Estate stood firm. It was obvious that the public and increasing numbers from the other two Estates were on its side. The king realized that he had to show that he accepted this change in mood, or else he might face an outright revolt. On 27 June, Louis ordered all the representatives of the First and Second Estates to join the National Assembly, which then called itself the National Constituent Assembly.

The French Guard (supporting the National Assembly) opens fire on German soldiers brought in and paid for by Louis XVI.

Excerpt from the king's address
In many of the most important issues, such as debating and
passing laws on taxes, Louis had to give in to the Third Estate.
However, this excerpt from his address to the National
Assembly shows how keen he was to keep the estates separate.

The king wants the ancient distinction
between the three Estates to be kept
completely, as an essential part of his
kingdom. He wants the elected members of
the three Estates to represent the nation.
The members will discuss proposals as
separate groups, and will only discuss
proposals together with the approval of the
king. Therefore, the king declares illegal
all the decisions made by members of the
Third Estate since the 17th of this month.

It is I, at present, who am doing
everything for the happiness of my people.
I order you, gentlemen, to separate
immediately, and to go tomorrow morning
to your separate meeting rooms in order
to start your meetings again. I order,
therefore, the grand master of ceremonies
to have the rooms prepared.

Storming the Bastille

The French people were in no mood for compromise. They wanted a complete victory for the representatives of the Third Estate, and they were furious that Louis XVI had dismissed Jacques Necker and brought in foreign troops. Unrest began to sweep across Paris, and the main targets were the symbols of the king's power. Full-scale rioting began on 12 July 1789. Two days later, the crowds turned on the Bastille, a royal prison. By this time there were only a few prisoners left in the Bastille, but it was still an important symbol of the cruel power of the king. The rioters stormed and took over the Bastille, freeing the prisoners and capturing those who had guarded it.

More than any other event, the storming of the Bastille has come to represent the dramatic start of the French Revolution. It remains a powerful memory among French people, and Bastille Day (14 July) is still the major national holiday in France.

The storming of the mighty Bastille on 14 July 1789 signalled the start of the sweeping changes that would shake France.

Louis de Flue's experience

A Swiss officer named Louis de Flue was one of the foreign troops brought into Paris by Louis XVI. He was one of the defenders of the Bastille, although – as this passage shows – the soldiers were not strong enough to stop those who stormed the royal prison. Also, many of the soldiers were in no mood to fight citizens who shared their political hopes.

About three o'clock in the afternoon, a troop of armed citizens mixed with some soldiers came to attack. They entered without difficulty into the courtyard. They cut the chains holding the drawbridge, and it fell open; this operation was easily carried out because the governor had ordered his troops not to fire before having warned them to leave, which we could not do while they were still at such a distance from the fortress.

After having easily dropped the bridge, the **besiegers** easily knocked down the door with axes and entered into the courtyard, where the governor went to meet them. He asked them what they wanted, and the general cry went up to 'Lower the bridges!' The governor responded that he could not, and he withdrew, ordering his troops to take up defensive positions. The sieging forces brought their cannons to the gates. I stationed my men to the left of the gate.

I waited for the moment when the governor [was] to carry out his threat, and I was very surprised to see him send four people to the gates to open them and to lower the bridges. The crowd entered right away and disarmed us in an instant in the castle, documents were thrown from the windows and everything was **pillaged**.

Confusion and order

The storming of the Bastille and other events in July 1789 triggered a burst of violence throughout France. Rioting crowds broke into prisons, attacked well-dressed people whom they accused of being **aristocrats**, and marched through the streets making demands. Normal activities came to a standstill. Nicola Rualt, a member of an armed patrol set up to protect property, wrote: 'We could not contain the people's fury… It is not the moment to reason with them.'

Provisional governments were formed to maintain order, and their rule was enforced by a new group of soldiers called the National Guard. The National Guard was placed under the command of the Marquis de Lafayette, a Frenchman who was one of the heroes of the American Revolution. This choice of a leader was a clever one. Lafayette was an admired and respected military leader. Even though he had helped the Americans to win their War of Independence, Lafayette was not comfortable with some of the **radical** political ideas that were spreading through France. He was someone who might be able to 'contain the people's fury'.

Another popular hero of the times was Jean-Sylvain Bailly, a distinguished scientist. He was the first President of the National Assembly, and he also became mayor of Paris on 15 July 1789. He knew that the mood in the country was violent, and that people's expectations had changed forever.

King Louis XVI was shocked by the rising tide of revolt. He withdrew the troops that he had put in place in Paris and other cities, and he recalled Jacques Necker to the government. He also made into law the decisions that had been taken by the provisional governments.

Jean-Sylvain Bailly, an astronomer, became the first mayor of Paris in 1789.

26 August:

I have already demanded that attention be focused on providing Paris with grain. I returned to the Assembly, and I asked that attention be given to providing the capital with food for the early winter months we can only obtain it from foreign sources. I saw that the grain bought by the government is running out. I thought that in a disastrous period – at the time of a good harvest, but one which will start being consumed two or three months earlier than usual – it was necessary to have a stockpile of food in reserve. This will prevent any cause or excuse for an uprising. Such a stockpile could only be obtained abroad. The cartloads of flour in our convoys are not only **pillaged** on the way by mobs, but are also pillaged in Paris by bakers who wait for them on the outskirts. Such disorder created two serious problems: the first is that the distribution of flour is unequal: one baker has too much, another not enough. The second is that the Paris market is poorly stocked, which upsets the public.

The Rights of Man

Despite the turmoil that gripped France, the representatives of the National Assembly never lost sight of their main task. From the outset, they had promised a **constitution** which would set out the rights and responsibilities of all French people. However, drawing up a constitution, and voting on it for approval, would take time. The French nation needed to have a clear idea of what the new constitution would do.

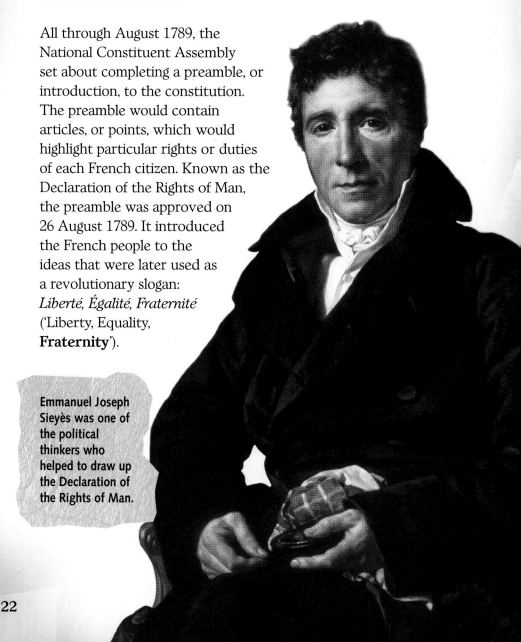

All through August 1789, the National Constituent Assembly set about completing a preamble, or introduction, to the constitution. The preamble would contain articles, or points, which would highlight particular rights or duties of each French citizen. Known as the Declaration of the Rights of Man, the preamble was approved on 26 August 1789. It introduced the French people to the ideas that were later used as a revolutionary slogan: *Liberté, Égalité, Fraternité* ('Liberty, Equality, **Fraternity**').

Emmanuel Joseph Sieyès was one of the political thinkers who helped to draw up the Declaration of the Rights of Man.

Art. 1. Men are born and remain free and equal in rights. Social distinctions may be based only upon the general good.

Art. 2. The aim of all political association is the preservation of the natural rights of man. These rights are liberty, property, security, and resistance to **oppression**.

Art. 4. Liberty consists in the freedom to do everything which hurts no one else. Hence, the exercise of the natural rights of each person has no limits except those which assure to the other members of the society the enjoyment of the same rights. These limits can only be decided by law.

Art. 9. Because all persons are believed to be innocent until proven guilty, if an arrest is necessary, all harshness is severely forbidden by law.

Art. 10. No one shall be arrested on account of his opinions, including his religious views, provided that their expression does not disturb the public order established by law.

Art. 11. The free communication of ideas and opinions is one of the most precious of the rights of man. Every citizen may, accordingly, speak, write and print with freedom, but shall be responsible for such abuses of this freedom, as defined by law.

Defining the new country

After nearly a year, the National Constituent Assembly finally completed work on a **constitution** for France. Using the Declaration of the Rights of Man as a starting point, the constitution spelled out exactly how laws should be passed, how representatives should be elected, how courts should operate and how other aspects of life in France should be conducted. Many **radical** French thinkers linked the king with everything that was bad and unfair about the old system. However, most French people, at that time, still believed that they should have a king.

The powers of the nobles and the **clergy** were another matter. Over the course of 1789–90, while the constitution was being drawn up, the Assembly passed a number of laws limiting the powers of the First and Second Estates. The most important of these laws, passed on 19 June 1790, got rid of **hereditary** nobility and titles. The idea of a hereditary nobility was unacceptable because it was **undemocratic** and it was not in keeping with the notion of equality. The new laws meant that the nobles would be citizens like other French people. The king approved the first draft of the constitution on 14 July 1790, at ceremonies in Paris, attended by representatives from all parts of the nation.

Many nobles, alarmed by attacks on their property and themselves, decided to leave France and settle in other European countries.

Decree of the National Constituent Assembly

The late eighteenth century in France was a time not only of revolution, but of **Enlightenment**. Many of the new laws passed by the National Constituent Assembly removed the outward signs of noble power and privilege.

Decree Abolishing Hereditary Nobility and Titles

(19 June 1790)

Art. 1.   The National Constituent Assembly decrees that hereditary nobility is forever abolished. Consequently, the titles of Prince, Duke, Count, Marquis, Viscount, Vidame, Baron, Knight, Lord, Squire, Noble and all other similar titles shall neither be accepted by, nor granted to upon, anyone at all.

Art. 2.   A citizen may assume only the real name of his family. [Until then, nobles would take the name of the region they owned as their last name.]

Art. 3.   The titles of Your Royal Highness and Your Royal Highnesses shall not be granted to any group or individual, nor shall the titles of Excellency, Highness, Eminence, Grace and so on. However, no citizen can take the liberty of attacking either monuments in churches or documents concerning families or properties.

Art. 4.   The present decree does not apply to foreigners.

Controlling the king

Life for Louis XVI was difficult in the first years of the French Revolution. His powers were limited with each new law passed by the National Constituent Assembly. Many revolutionaries feared that Louis would try to persuade foreign kings to crush the Revolution. Other European kings would welcome the chance to end the anti-royalist revolution in France, because they were afraid of it spreading to their own countries and reducing their power. As a result, Louis and his family were watched very closely by the new French government. The royal family tried to escape in June 1791, but were captured and returned. This attempted escape turned public opinion against the king even more.

On 17 July 1791, thousands of **republicans** gathered in Paris and demanded that the king be overthrown. Republicans believed that their leaders should be elected. Troops opened fire on the republican demonstrators. The bloodshed widened the gap between the republican and **conservative** sections of the population. After suspending Louis for a brief period, the **moderate** majority of the National Constituent Assembly reinstated the king. They hoped that his continued presence would prevent foreign powers (including Britain) invading on his behalf.

The bloodshed of 17 July 1791, when many protestors were shot dead, divided France even further.

Today, when his only payment for so many sacrifices consists of mainly seeing the monarchy destroyed, and total chaos taking the place of law, the king, having protested against all the laws passed during his captivity, believes it is his duty to place before Frenchmen and the entire universe an account of his behaviour and that of the government which has established itself in the kingdom.

But the more sacrifices the king made for the benefit of his people, the more the rebels laboured to paint the monarchy in the most false and hateful colours.

The calling of the Estates-General, the doubling of the representatives of the Third Estate, the king's efforts to eliminate all difficulties which might delay the meeting of the Estates-General, all the reductions which the king made in his personal expenses, all the sacrifices which he made for his people in the session of 23 June, all his efforts, all his generosity, all his devotion to his people – all have been misjudged, all have been misrepresented.

Calls for war

Early 1792 saw French people of all political sides calling for war. Many French nobles had fled the country and sought the aid of foreign powers to crush the Revolution. Some of those countries, such as Britain and Austria, were **monarchies**, and felt threatened by the spread of revolutionary ideas from France.

Within France, there were calls for war from two directions. Supporters of the king welcomed the idea of a foreign invasion that would restore the old system. **Republicans** believed such an invasion was likely, and that France needed to strike first to defend itself and to protect the gains of the Revolution.

On 20 April 1792, the **Legislative** Assembly – which, by this time, had replaced the National Constituent Assembly – declared war on the Austrian part of the **Holy Roman Empire**. This began the series of conflicts known as the French revolutionary wars. Feelings were running high and the public believed that the Revolution was soon to be tested to the limit.

Eager to defend the revolutionary gains of recent years, French troops (in blue) marched into battle against Austria.

'La Marseillaise'

'La Marseillaise', the French national anthem, was composed on 24 April 1792 by Claude-Joseph Rouget de Lisle. Volunteer soldiers from the southern city of Marseilles sang it as they entered Paris. The words of this stirring song (the first verse is below in both French and English) echo the strong feelings of those who vowed to defend revolutionary France.

Allons enfants de la Patrie
Le jour de gloire est arrivé!
Contre nous, de la tyrannie,
L'étandard sanglant est levé,
l'étandard sanglant est levé,
Entendez-vous, dans les campagnes.
Mugir ces soldats féroces?
Ils viennent jusque dans vos bras
Egorger vos fils et vos compagnes.

Let us arise, children of our motherland
Our day of glory has arrived!
Against us, a sign of tyranny,
The bloody flag is raised,
The bloody flag is raised.
Do you hear in the countryside
The roar of these fierce soldiers?
They come right into our midst
To cut the throats of our sons,
  our wives and kin.

The 'September massacres'

By the summer of 1792, France was at war with a number of European enemies (notably Austria, Great Britain and Prussia) known as the Allies. The French suffered a series of defeats and the Allied commander, the Duke of Brunswick, threatened to destroy Paris if the royal family was mistreated. Far from moving the people to protect the royal family, this threat caused many French people to view the king as siding with the enemy. On 10 August 1792, a group of **radical** Parisians and volunteer soldiers stormed the Tuileries, the palace where the king lived, and massacred the king's Swiss guard. Louis XVI and his family fled to the nearby hall of the **Legislative** Assembly, which promptly suspended the king and placed him in **confinement**.

The radicals, led by the lawyer Georges Jacques Danton, also took over the Parisian government, and soon gained control of the Legislative Assembly. After new elections, it became known as the National Convention. Between 2 and 6 September, more than 1000 supporters of the king and suspected traitors were rounded up and killed. Even supporters of the Revolution were at risk, if they were judged to be not radical enough or had behaved suspiciously in the eyes of the radicals. The prisoners had mock 'trials', often led by drunken troublemakers who stirred public fears about traitors helping foreign forces. These killings became known as the 'September massacres'.

The storming of the king's palace, the Tuileries, marked the beginning of the end for Louis XVI, and for the monarchy in France.

Article from *The Times*
The British government, along with most members of the British press, opposed the French Revolution. This account, from *The Times* of 10 September 1792, paints a vivid picture of the violence of the 'September massacres'.

The Times

10 September 1792

The number of **clergy** found in the Carmelite Convent was about 220. They were handed out of the prison door two by two into the Rue Vaugerard, where their throats were cut. Their bodies were fixed on **pikes** and exhibited to the wretched victims who were next to suffer. The mangled bodies of others are piled against the houses in the streets; and in the quarters of Paris near to which the prisons are, the carcasses lie scattered in hundreds, diffusing **pestilence** all around.

The streets of Paris, strewed with the carcasses of the mangled victims, are become so familiar to the sight, that they are passed by and trod on without any particular notice. The mob think no more of killing a fellow-creature, who is not even an object of suspicion, than wanton boys would of killing a cat or a dog. We have it from a Gentleman who has been but too often an eye witness to the fact. In the massacre last week, every person who had the appearance of a gentleman, whether stranger or not, was run through the body with a pike. He was of course an **aristocrat**, and that was a sufficient crime. A ring, a watch chain, a handsome pair of buckles, a new coat, or a good pair of boots in a word, every thing which marked the appearance of a gentleman, and which the mob fancied, was sure to cost the owner his life. EQUALITY was the pistol, and PLUNDER the object.

The king is dead

The National Convention, formed after the 1792 elections represented a new, and more **radical**, phase of the French Revolution. Its representatives were elected through **universal suffrage** which meant that every man had the right to vote. The Convention abolished the remaining powers of the monarchy, and declared a **Republic** for the first time. From this point onwards, the nation's leaders would always be elected. However, simply having Louis XVI overthrown was still not enough for many people, who thought he would be free to gain foreign support. These people would only be satisfied if all royalty were eliminated – and the king with it.

The Convention accused Louis of **treason**. On 15 January 1793, by an almost **unanimous** vote, the Convention found the king guilty. Shortly afterwards, by a vote of 380 to 310, the representatives approved the death penalty. It was a close margin – there were still many who did not want the king to be executed. At eight o'clock on 21 January 1793, a guard of 1200 soldiers arrived to escort the former king on a two-hour carriage ride to his place of execution. The execution was swift, with Louis's head severed from his body with the **guillotine** – soon to become a symbol of terror and death in Paris. There was no turning back for the Revolution now.

Louis XVI faced his executioners with dignity. His beheading was a turning point in the French Revolution – France was now a Republic.

The path leading to the scaffold was extremely rough and difficult to pass; the King was obliged to lean on my arm, and I feared for a moment that his courage might fail; but what was my astonishment, when arrived at the last step, I felt that he suddenly let go my arm, and I saw him cross with a firm foot the breadth of the whole scaffold and in a voice so loud... I heard him pronounce distinctly these memorable words: 'I die innocent of all the crimes laid to my charge; I pardon those who have occasioned my death; and I pray to God that the blood you are going to shed may never be visited on France.'

He was proceeding, when a man on horseback, in the national uniform, and with a ferocious cry, ordered the drums to beat. Many voices were at the same time heard encouraging the executioners. They dragged him under the axe of the guillotine, which with one stroke severed his head from his body. The youngest of the guards immediately seized the head, and showed it to the people. At first, an awful silence prevailed; at length, some cries of 'Vive la Republique!' were heard. By degrees, the voices multiplied and, in less than ten minutes, this cry, a thousand times repeated, became the universal shout of the multitude, and every hat was in the air.

Wars on all fronts

The execution of Louis XVI was a milestone in the French Revolution. His death showed the French people – and other European nations – that there was no turning back. The effect was very powerful, and many Europeans felt that revolutionary ideas would soon spread from France and lead to violence across Europe. The major European powers decided to take action, and planned to attack France. By March 1793, France saw these enemies gathering at its northern and eastern borders. An Austrian army captured Aachen (a German city controlled by the French), and another army – made up of British, Dutch and German troops – gathered in the Netherlands.

At about the same time, a new threat to the Revolution developed inside the borders of France. **Royalists** and religious leaders stirred up the population of the Vendée, a region in western France, into outright revolt against the Revolutionary government. They called for a return to royal rule, and for the rights of the Catholic Church to be restored.

The National Convention ordered 300,000 new **conscripts** to defend France against outside invaders – and to defend the Revolution against its enemies within France itself. Would they be enough?

Georges Jacques Danton, who had swept to the main stage of power during the 'September massacres' (see pages 30–31), was now at the heart of the problems facing France. He was a powerful speaker and political leader, who could influence people's opinions with a carefully chosen phrase. As a government leader, he also needed to judge France's real position in the outside world. So, in early March 1793, he went on a secret mission to Belgium to judge the threat. He returned on 10 March to find Paris in a state of near panic. Danton realized that the new French government faced a deadly threat, but he also knew that France was sure to lose if the people continued to panic.

Danton's speech
Danton gave many stirring calls to arms in defence of the French Revolution. In the following extract of his speech to the National Convention, he plays on his own reputation for violence to urge Frenchmen to follow his example.

See, citizens, the fair destinies that await you. What! You have a whole nation as a lever and you have not yet upturned the whole world! To do this, we need firmness and character; and, to tell the truth, we lack it. I put to one side all passions. They are all strangers to me apart from the passion I have for the public good.

Georges Jacques Danton was a lawyer and fiery **orator**, who urged his countrymen to fight for France.

When the enemy was at the gates of Paris, I said to those in charge: 'Your discussions are shameful; I can see only the enemy. (applause from the Convention). You tire me by your squabbling, in place of occupying yourselves with the safety of the republic! You are all traitors to our country!' I said to them: 'What do I care for my reputation? Let France be free, even though my name is cursed!' What do I care that I am called a 'blood-drinker'? Well, let us drink the blood of the enemies of humanity, if need be; but let us struggle, let us achieve freedom.'

The Committee of Public Safety

France listened to Danton's words and prepared to face its foreign enemies. But the home front was divided between **radicals**, who favoured immediate sweeping changes, and the more cautious **moderates**. Their disputes in the National Convention weakened France's ability to make quick decisions. As a result, on 6 April 1793, the Convention established the nine-member (later changed to twelve-member) Committee of Public Safety, as the main governing body of the **Republic**. This move marked the beginning of another, yet even more radical phase of the Revolution: hard-liners had control of the new ruling group.

The Committee of Public Safety helped to bring calm to the economy, and it began to form a national army. One of its main aims was to deal with French anti-revolutionary groups, mainly in the south and west. It set up revolutionary **tribunals** to deal with suspected 'traitors'. Many of the accused actually supported the Revolution – but not enough, in the eyes of the radicals. Crowds filled the rooms for some trials, as famous people awaited their fate. Those who were convicted faced the **guillotine**.

The fearsome killing machine was invented by Joseph Guillotin. Its purpose was to quickly and efficiently execute the many French citizens thought to be enemies of the Revolution.

J.G. Millingen's account

In October 1793, Englishman J.G. Millingen witnessed the trial of more than a dozen suspected **counter-revolutionaries** at the Paris Revolutionary Tribunal. Here he describes the progress of the condemned on the way to their execution.

The process of execution was also a sad and heart-rending spectacle. In the middle of the Place de la Revolution (a great space in central Paris, now known as the Place de la Concorde, or 'Peace Square') was erected a guillotine, in front of a colossal statue of Liberty, represented seated on a rock, a Phrygian cap (a floppy cap, which revolutionaries used as a symbol of liberty) on her head, a spear in her hand, the other reposing on a shield. On one side of the **scaffold** were a sufficient number of carts, with large baskets painted red, to receive the heads and bodies of the victims.

Those carrying the condemned moved on slowly to the foot of the guillotine; the culprits were led out in turn, and, if necessary, supported by two of the executioner's attendants... but their assistance was rarely required. Most of these unfortunates ascended the scaffold with a determined step – many of them looked up firmly on the mincing instrument of death (the writer's description of the sharp and menacing guillotine), beholding for the last time the rays of the glorious sun, beaming on the polished axe.

The Reign of Terror

As 1793 turned into 1794, the Committee of Public Safety and its revolutionary **tribunals** stepped up the hunt for those that they believed threatened the Revolution. Maximilien Robespierre became the dominant member of the Committee. Robespierre was single-minded about protecting the gains of the Revolution. He was pitiless towards those he regarded as enemies. It seemed that he would stop at nothing – even mass executions – to achieve his aim.

No one was safe in what came to be known as 'the Reign of Terror'. **Moderates** who opposed the execution of Louis XVI were branded as traitors. Among them was the Marquis de Lafayette, who had supported the American Revolution and played a public role in French events after 1789. When he was denounced as a traitor, he gave himself up to the Austrian army that was poised to attack France. On 16 October 1793, Queen Marie Antoinette was executed, and 21 leading moderates were beheaded on 31 October. This began a deadly wave of trials and executions lasting more than a year. Revolutionary tribunals were responsible for the execution of almost 17,000 French citizens. The victims of the Reign of Terror totalled approximately 40,000, including those who died in overcrowded, disease-ridden prisons, and rebels executed on the field of battle.

Marie Antoinette was judged by the Revolutionary Tribunal Court in October 1793, before being sentenced to death, like her husband Louis XVI.

The writings of Robespierre

Robespierre knew that many people accused him of leading a **despotic** government. As this extract from early 1794 reveals, he believed that terror was an acceptable weapon in the battle to preserve the French Revolution.

It has been said that terror is the basis of despotic government. Does your government, therefore, resemble despotism? Yes, just as the sword that gleams in the hands of the heroes of liberty resembles that with which the supporters of **tyranny** are armed. Let the despot govern by terror his brutalized subjects; he is right, as a despot. Subdue by terror the enemies of liberty, and you will be right, as founders of the **Republic**. The government of the revolution is liberty's despotism against tyranny. Is force made only to protect crime? And is the thunderbolt not destined to strike the heads of the proud? 'Indulgence for the royalists,' cry certain men, 'Mercy for the villains!' No! mercy for the innocent, mercy for the weak, mercy for the unfortunate, mercy for humanity.

Society owes protection only to peaceable citizens; the only citizens in the Republic are the **republicans**. For the Republic, the **royalists**, the **conspirators**, are only strangers or, rather, enemies. This terrible war waged by liberty against tyranny — is it not indivisible? Are the enemies within not the allies of the enemies without?

The fall of Robespierre

Under the leadership of Robespierre, the government introduced many changes to France. The Catholic Church and other organized religions lost even more power and property. Even the calendar was changed. The year 1793 became known as Year I, because that is when the **Republic** was declared. (The year actually began on 22 September 1792 and ended on 21 September 1793.) New names of months suggested Nature rather than ancient gods.

Running alongside all of these social changes was the continuing violence of the Reign of Terror. By mid-1794, French Revolutionary forces began to achieve a number of military successes. Some people began to question Robespierre's leadership, wondering whether all the violence was still necessary. Louis Freron, in his newspaper *L'Orateur du Peuple*, began accusing Robespierre of being a **dictator**. Many others echoed this view. Robespierre's time ran out suddenly on 27 July 1794, when the National Convention voted to arrest Robespierre. He and 98 of his followers were seized and beheaded the next day.

Robespierre and his followers were seized and arrested on 29 July (known in the Revolutionary Calendar as 'the Ninth Thermidor'). They were executed the following day.

Pierre-Toussaint Durand de Maillane's account

Pierre-Toussaint Durand de Maillane, a **moderate** representative, describes what happened in the Convention Hall on 27 July 1794. Robespierre faced an organized attack by other members of the Committee of Public Safety, and was condemned by the National Convention.

Meanwhile, the Reign of Terror was reaching its end. Robespierre had become unbearable, even to his own supporters. The members of the committees were in a power struggle with him, and were afraid that, sooner or later, they would become his victims. When faced with his **tyranny** in the Convention, everyone whimpered, not daring to attack him. Several of those who had been threatened could no longer sleep, so, to defend themselves, they plotted against Robespierre. But how to go about overthrowing him? Robespierre was in charge of all of the Parisian authorities and counted Henriot, the commander of the Armed Forces, among his devoted followers. Only a ruling from the Convention could fell this giant.

Robespierre went up to the **rostrum**. The only words that could be heard were: 'Down with the **tyrant**! Arrest him!' Robespierre turned to us and said: 'Deputies of the Right, men of honour, men of virtue, let me speak, since the **assassins** will not.' He hoped to receive this favour as a reward for the protection he had given us before. But our party was decided. There was no answer, just dead silence until the debate over the decision to arrest Robespierre and his supporters, for which we all voted in favour, which made the decision **unanimous**.

The Directory

By 1795, the Revolutionary armies had restored peace to the French borders, but, once again, turmoil threatened to sweep across France itself. The National Convention (now controlled by the **moderate** and **conservative** representatives, which had condemned Robespierre) could not prevent new outbreaks of **radical** demonstrations.

On 22 August 1795, the Convention adopted a new **constitution**, which tried to find a balance between the radical and conservative forces to maintain national unity. In a move to satisfy radicals, the new constitution granted full citizenship (and voting rights) to all men aged 21 and over. But only property owners or men in full-time work could stand for political office. The constitution also established new sources of power within France. A five-member Directory had central, or **executive**, power (like that of a modern prime minister or president). Two elected bodies had **legislative** power (like that of a parliament or congress) which meant that they could pass new laws. These were: the Council of Elders, with 250 members, and the Council of the Five Hundred.

This system seemed to work well on paper, but soon there were divisions within the government. Demonstrations and rebellions from the general public also developed. Some of these rebellions, such as that of the radical François Noël Babeuf, threatened to overthrow the government itself. Other people simply wanted to be able to live in peace and to afford their next meal – no matter what type of government ruled the country.

As well as dealing with political attacks from all fronts, the Directory had a much more serious problem — keeping France supplied with food and other essential goods. A British naval **blockade** prevented France from getting these goods from overseas, and much of the food produced within France went to the armies. The government had to restrict the sale of basic foods, candles and firewood just as the first frosts of a severe winter froze the country at the beginning of November 1795. Some of these goods were available at hugely increased prices in Paris and other cities through the **black market**. Elsewhere, people faced starvation.

Célestin Guillard de Floriban's diary

This brief diary account of Parisian Célestin Guillard de Floriban captures the atmosphere in the French capital during the winter of 1795–6.

The price of everything is excessive. No more order, no more supervision, everybody free to sell what he has for whatever he wants. It really seems that the time has come at last to die of hunger and cold, lacking everything. Great God, what a **Republic**! and the worst of it is, one can't tell when or how it will end. Everybody is dying of hunger.

François Noël Babeuf was a radical, who believed that the Revolution had not gone far enough. His calls for equal distribution of land and income were a great threat to the Directory.

The rise of Napoleon

The Directory governed France for the next four years, but its rivalries and divisions continued to threaten peaceful government within France. However, France was making great progress in its activities abroad. A little-known officer from the French island of Corsica, Napoleon Bonaparte, was an outstanding military leader in France's time of need.

In 1793, Napoleon drove out a British fleet from the French port of Toulon and, in 1795, he crushed a disturbance in Paris. By 1796, he had been promoted several times, and he commanded the French army in Italy. He defeated four Austrian generals in succession and forced Austria to make peace. Napoleon's string of successes continued in the eastern Mediterranean region; in 1798, he conquered Turkish-controlled Egypt, and defeated the Turks again in 1799.

Seeing Napoleon as a possible national leader, several French politicians overthrew the troubled Directory on 9 November 1799. They launched yet another **constitution** on 24 December 1799. This constitution gave power to a body called the Consulate, but real power went to the First Consul. The man chosen to be First Consul was General Napoleon Bonaparte.

Napoleon Bonaparte became a national hero after his military victories. After so many years of turmoil France was ready for a strong leader.

Napoleon's statement

Just how Napoleon achieved power on 9 November 1799 is a matter of disagreement even today. But Napoleon knew that he needed the support of the French people. His first public statement, the following day, provides his version of events.

10 November 1799

On my return to Paris, I found division among all the authorities, and agreement upon only one point: that the constitution was half destroyed and could not save liberty. All parties came to me, confided to me their plans, disclosed their secrets, and asked for my support. I refused to be one party's man. The Council of Elders summoned me, and I went. An outline for general restoration had been planned by the men who the nation has become accustomed to regarding as the defenders of liberty, equality and property. The Council of Elders gave me control over the forces necessary to ensure its independence. I believed it my duty to accept the command, for my fellow citizens, for the soldiers being killed in our armies, and for the national glory acquired at the cost of their blood.

I appeared before the Council of Five-Hundred, just as I had before the Elders, alone, unarmed, my head uncovered, and was applauded. I had come to remind the majority of its will, and to assure them of their power. Deputies, armed with knives, rushed at me. At the same moment, cries of 'outlaw' were raised against me, the defender of the law. It was the fierce cry of **assassins** against the power that was destined to suppress them.

Guards took the armed deputies away. The majority, freed from their attacks, returned peaceably into the meeting hall, listened to the proposals on behalf of public safety and drafted the resolution which is to become the new law of the Republic.

Transforming the Revolution

During the rule of the Consulate, Napoleon Bonaparte carried through a series of reforms that were begun during the Revolution. He established the Bank of France, strengthened the school system, made government jobs open to all who were qualified for them and established a system of justice known as the Napoleonic Code. Many of the **radical**, **democratic** goals of the Revolution were put aside, but France was strengthened at home. France also launched a series of military campaigns and, by 1806, it controlled much of western Europe.

Napoleon became more and more powerful. He changed the **constitution** to give himself even more powers than he had as First Consul. In 1802, he became First Consul for life (dismissing the Revolution's idea of elected leadership). Two years later, he had himself declared Emperor. This political situation was far removed from the ideals of the Revolution, but many French people believed that their life was better under Napoleon. Also, they felt that Napoleon had preserved many of the most important achievements of the Revolution in the areas of education, justice and business.

The Battle of Trafalgar in 1805 was one of the major naval battles in history. The British, under Admiral Horatio Nelson, defeated the combined French and Spanish fleet, and ruined Napoleon's plans to invade England.

Napoleon's measures against the British

In 1806, Napoleon announced the Continental System, a series of measures to stop British goods from reaching Europe. Britain had opposed the Revolution and had formed several alliances to stop Napoleon's progress. It had **blockaded** French-controlled territories and Napoleon decided to use the same tactic against Britain.

From our imperial camp at Berlin, 21 November 1806

Napoleon, Emperor of the French and King of Italy, in consideration of the fact:

1. That England does not recognize the system of international law universally observed by all civilized nations

5. That England's monstrous abuse of the right of blockade has no other aim than to prevent communication among the nations and to raise the commerce and the industry of England upon the ruins of that of the continent.

7. That this policy of England, worthy of the earliest stages of barbarism, has profited that power to the **detriment** of every other nation.

We have consequently decreed and do decree that which follows:

Art. I. The British Isles are declared to be in a state of blockade.

Art. II. All commerce and all correspondence with the British Isles are forbidden.

Art. III. Every individual who is an English subject, of whatever state or condition he may be, who shall be discovered in any country occupied by our troops or by those of our allies, shall be made a prisoner of war.

Art. IV. All warehouses, merchandise or property of whatever kind belonging to a subject of England shall be regarded as a lawful prize.

Art. V. Trade in English goods is prohibited, and all goods belonging to England or coming from her factories or her colonies are declared a lawful prize.

Legacy of the Revolution

The abolition of the **monarchy** was the most direct result of the French Revolution. The Revolution was also responsible for destroying the **feudal** privileges of the nobles. With these major powers swept away, the Revolution (despite its twists and turns) transformed French society. A series of revolutionary laws saw that wealth and property were distributed more equally within the country. With these laws in place, France became the European nation with the largest proportion of small independent landowners. Other revolutionary reforms included abolishing imprisonment for debt, introducing the metric system and establishing a national educational system.

The ideals of the Revolution, often expressed with the words 'Liberty, Equality and **Fraternity**', have inspired freedom seekers for more than two centuries. Dozens of countries have adopted versions of France's 'tricolour' flag as a tribute to those who struggled for **democracy** in France from 1789 onwards.

The writer Victor Hugo was the son of a general in Napoleon's army. He grew up with a sense of pride in the achievements of the French Revolution.

While **exiled** from France for his **radical** political views, Victor Hugo wrote many of his greatest works. His writings which include *The Hunchback of Notre Dame* and *Les Misérables*, reveal his deep sympathy with the lives of ordinary people.

Out of this chaos of shadow spread immense rays of light parallel to the eternal laws – rays that have remained on the horizon, visible forever in the heaven of the peoples, and which are, one, Justice; another, Tolerance; another, Goodness; another, Right; another, Truth; another, Love.

The National Convention proclaimed this grand truth: 'The liberty of each citizen ends where the liberty of another citizen commences,' – which comprises in two lines all human social law. It abolished slavery. It proclaimed civic joint responsibility. It decreed free education. It organized national education by the normal school of Paris; central schools in the chief towns; primary schools in the communes. It created the academies of music and the museums. It decreed the unity of weights and measures, and the unity of calculation by the decimal system.

Of the eleven thousand, two hundred and ten decrees which came from the Convention, a third had a political aim; and twothirds had a human aim. It declared that universal morality was the basis of society, and that universal conscience was the basis of law.

What have we learnt from the French Revolution?

The French Revolution was full of **contradictions**, lurching back and forth from **radical** reform to **conservative** reaction. Despite its unpredictable nature, the Revolution had a force of its own. Certain events meant there would be no turning back. The Third Estate, by becoming the dominant power in the National Assembly, made sure that its voice would ring the loudest in years to come. By overcoming the symbolic Bastille, the revolutionaries knew that the king's power could be overturned. Louis XVI's execution in 1793 was almost inevitable, as was the anti-revolutionary response of other European monarchs. It was not surprising that Robespierre and his allies would inflict the Reign of Terror in an attempt to stifle any protests against the new **Republic**.

French revolutionary ideals also took root elsewhere. The Tree of Liberty being cut down in this painting had marked the founding of a short-lived Republic in Naples in 1799.

Later still, Napoleon's rise to power as a forceful figure of central power was the next step. We can look back at all of these stages and see patterns. These patterns appeared in later violent revolutions – especially in Russia and China. Since 1798, the revolutionary cries of 'Liberty, Equality and **Fraternity**' have rung out, inspiring nations and people around the world.

Alexis de Tocqueville's view

The nobleman Alexis de Tocqueville (1805–59) was a historian, social critic and politician who wrote: *The Old Régime and the French Revolution* (1856). In the extract on page 51 he describes the attraction of the Revolution even after nearly seven decades.

I have always believed that the effort of making France a free nation (in the true sense of the word) was noble and bold. I find it to be bolder every day, but at the same time to be nobler, so that, if I could be reborn, I would prefer to risk myself completely in this daring adventure than to bend under the necessity of being a servant. Will others be happier than we have been? I do not know Changes that were made in the social state, in the institutions, in the mind and in the social customs of the French as the Revolution progressed – that is my subject. For seeing it well, I have up to now found only one way; that is to live, in some manner, each moment of the Revolution with the **contemporaries** by reading, not what has been said of them or what they said of themselves since, but what they themselves were saying then, and, as much as possible, by discovering what they were really thinking. The minor writings of the time, private correspondence are even more effective in reaching this goal than the debates of the assemblies. By the route I am taking, I am reaching the goal I am setting for myself, which is to place myself successively in the midst of the time. But the process is so slow that I often despair of it. Yet, is there any other?

Alexis de Tocqueville had lived for years in the newly independent United States. He was in a good position to compare the contributions made by the two revolutions – in America and in his homeland.

Timeline

1789	5 May: Meeting of the Estates-General
	17 June: National Assembly declared
	20 June: Tennis Court Oath
	14 July: Storming of the Bastille
	27 August: Declaration of the Rights of Man
	5–6 October: Outbreak of the Paris mob. **Liberal constitution** retains monarchy
1790	19 June: All **aristocratic**, **hereditary** titles are abolished
	14 July: Constitution accepted by the king
1791	20–5 June: Flight of the king
	30 September: National Constituent Assembly ends
	1 October: **Legislative** Assembly meets
1792	7 February: Alliance of Austria and Prussia against revolutionary France
	10 August: Storming of the Tuileries
	2–6 September: The September massacres
	21 September: National Convention meets. Abolition of the **monarchy**
	December: Trial of Louis XVI before the National Convention
1793	21 January: Execution of Louis XVI
	1 February: War declared against Great Britain, Holland and Spain
	March: **Royalist** revolt in the Vendée region of western France
	April: Committee of Public Security gains real power
	16 October: Execution of Marie Antoinette, beginning of the Reign of Terror
	December: Retreat of the Allies across the Rhine
1794	5 April: Execution of Georges Danton and his allies
	27 July: Fall of Robespierre (9 Thermidor)
1795	1 April: Bread riots in Paris
	22 August: Constitution of 1795
	5 October: Napoleon crushes disturbance in Paris
	26 October: National Convention terminated
1796	10 May: Battle of Lodi (Napoleon in Italy)
1797	17 October: Treaty of Campo Formio (Austria forced to recognize French gains in Italy)
1798	April: Helvetic Republic proclaimed in Switzerland
	21 July: Battle of the Pyramids (Napoleons defeats Turks in Egypt)
1799	24 August: Napoleon leaves Egypt
	9 November: The '18 Brumaire' overthrow of the Directory
	24 December: Constitution of the Year VIII: guarantees Napoleon almost unlimited powers as First Consul
1802	27 March: Peace of Amiens ends European fighting for 14 months
1804	Napoleon crowns himself Emperor of France
1805	21 October: Napoleon's fleet defeated by Great Britain's Royal Navy under the command of Lord Nelson at the Battle of Trafalgar
1805–6	French victories at Austerlitz (1805) and Jena (1806) drive Austria, Prussia and Russia out of European wars

Find out more

Books & websites

The French Revolution, Fiona MacDonald, (Evans Books, 2001)
Turning Pounts: The Fall of the Bastille, Ross Stewart, (Heinemann Library, 2001)
The French Revolution, 1789–94, Martin Whittock, (Hodder Education, 2001)

Go exploring! Log onto Heinemann's online history resource at
www.heinemannexplore.co.uk

www.historyteacher.net/APEuroCourse/ApEuro_Main_Weblinks_Page.htm
This site has a variety of primary sources and several sound files for downloading

www.fordham.edu/halsall/mod/modsbook13.html
This site has a wide range of primary source documents from the French
Revolution, along with links to other events of the eighteenth century.

http://chnm.gmu.edu/revolution Liberty, Equality, Fraternity
This well-presented site has more than 300 text documents from the French
Revolution. It also contains a useful search engine for locating specific texts.

List of primary sources

The author and publisher gratefully acknowledge the following publications and
websites from which written sources in the book are drawn. In some cases the
wording or sentence structure has been simplified to make the material more
appropriate for a school readership

P.9 Marie Antoinette: www.fordham.edu/halsall/mod/1773marieantonette.html
P.11 Articles from the cahiers: history.hanover.edu/texts/cahiers3.html
P.13 Arthur Young: *The Faber Book of Reportage*: Ed John Carey (Faber & Faber, 1987)
P.15 Emmanuel-Joseph Sieyès: http://www.fordham.edu/halsall/mod/sieyes.html
P.17 Louis XVI: chnm.gmu.edu/revolution/d/303/
P.19 Louis de Flue: chnm.gmu.edu/revolution/d/383/
P.21 Jean-Sylvain Bailly: www.woodberry.org/acad/hist/FRWEB/ MARCH/documents/bailly.htm
P.23 Declaration of the Rights of Man: www.hrcr.org/docs/frenchdec.html
P.25 Decree of the National Constituent Assembly: www.chnm.gmu.edu/revolution/a/367/
P.27 King's Declaration: www.historyguide.org/intellect/varennes.html
P.29 'La Marseillaise': www.geocities.com/revolutioninfrance/culture.html
P.31 The Times: *The Faber Book of Reportage*: Ed John Carey (Faber & Faber, 1987)
P.33 Henry Essex Edgeworth: *The Faber Book of Reportage*: Ed John Carey (Faber & Faber, 1987)
P.35 Georges Danton: *The Penguin Book of Historic Speeches*, 1995. Ed by Brian MacArthur
     (Viking, 1995)
P.37 J.G. Millingen: *The Faber Book of Reportage*: Ed John Carey (Faber & Faber, 1987)
P.39 Maximilien Robespierre: *The Faber Book of Reportage*: Ed John Carey (Faber & Faber, 1987)
P.41 Pierre-Toussaint Durand de Maillane: chnm.gmu.edu/revolution/d/441/
P.43 Celestin Guillard de Floriban: *Journal de Celestin Guillard de Floriban, bourgeois de Paris sous la
     Revolution*, ed R. Aubert (Paris, 1974), reprinted in *The Oxford History of the French Revolution*,
     William Doyle, (Oxford University Press, 1989)
P.45 Napoleon: chnm.gmu.edu/revolution/d/461/
P.47 Napoleon: chnm.gmu.edu/revolution/d/518/
P.49 Victor Hugo: chnm.gmu.edu/revolution/d/587/
P.51 Alexis de Tocqueville: chnm.gmu.edu/revolution/d/590

Glossary

aristocrat noble person who usually has wealth and a high social position

assassin someone hired to kill someone else

besieger part of a force that is trying to capture a fortress or other protected position

bias judgement that is influenced by personal opinion

black market illegal sale of restricted goods, often at high prices

blockade surrounding or blocking a place by an enemy to prevent entry and exit of supplies

censorship controlling what can be said in public or written

clergy priest, bishops and other religious people

colonist someone who has left their native land to settle in a territory controlled by their home country

confinement prevented from leaving a place, usually by soldiers or other security forces

conscript someone who has been forced into military service

conservative opposed to political change, or a person who holds these views

conspirator person who is linked with a secret plot

constitution written statement of a country's government outlining the rights and liberties of its people

contemporaries those who lived at the time

contradiction statement that seems at odds with accepted facts

counter-revolutionaries people who try to overthrow a revolutionary government and return a country to the old system

Dauphin eldest son of a king of France

deliberating discussing and arguing over before reaching a decision

democracy system of government that tries to represent all the people in a country fairly by giving as many people as possible the chance to vote

despotic governing with little or no concern for public opinion

detriment worsening

dictator leader who has total control, with no restrictions

dissolve (of a political group) to stop a session

Enlightenment period in the seventeenth and eighteenth centuries when writers and artists sought new ways to bring happiness and justice to the world

executive related to carrying out laws

exile being forced to live away from one's own country, often because of political beliefs that oppose the government

feudal system of land ownership in which a single rich land owner controls the lives of those who work on the land

Fraternity quality of being brotherly

guillotine machine for beheading people which has a large blade that slides down a channel on to a block

hereditary inherited at birth

Holy Roman Empire a Germanic empire in central Europe which lasted from AD800 until 1806

legislative having the power to create laws

legislature branch of a government in which representatives discuss and pass laws

liberal favouring change in society

moderate not extreme

monarchy government or a system of government where a country ruled by a king or royal family

oppression harsh behaviour (by a government or ruler) against the people

orator public speaker

pamphlets booklets written and distributed to support a political cause

pestilence harmful disease

pike weapon with a long wooden handle and a pointed metal head

pillage to rob violently

primary source original document describing a historical event or era

propaganda information that is meant to sway or change public opinion

provisional temporary

radical favouring extreme change in society, or a person who favours such change

republic system of government in which leaders are elected or chosen rather than hereditary

republicans people favouring a republican style of government

rostrum stand for public speaking

royalist person who supports monarchy

scaffold raised wooden platform used for the execution of criminals

secondary source historical record that is written by someone who was not present when an event took place

sovereign king or queen

treason crime of betraying one's country to a foreign (usually enemy) power

tribunal special court for trying political cases

tyranny rule by brute power

tyrant cruel or oppressive leader

unanimous with everyone agreeing

undemocratic system where leaders are not elected

universal suffrage system of voting in which every adult (or, in the eighteenth century, every adult male) has the right to vote

vengeful seeking to strike back at someone

Key events in the French Revolution

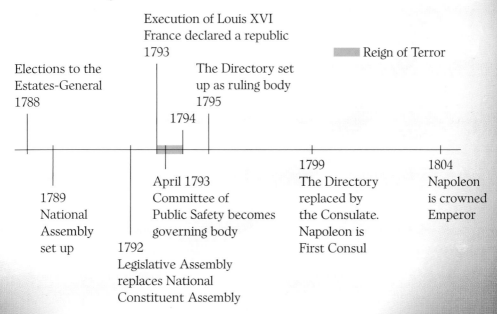

Index

American Revolution 4, 20, 51

Babeuf, François Noël 42, 43
Bailly, Jean-Sylvain 20, 21
Bastille 4, 5, 7, 18–19, 50
Britain 4, 28, 31, 42, 46, 47

calendar, revolutionary 40
Catholic Church 34, 40
clergy 8, 12, 14, 24, 31
Committee of Public Safety 36, 38, 41
constitution 5, 14, 22, 24, 42, 44, 46
Continental System 47
counter-revolutionaries 34, 36, 37

Danton, Georges Jacques 7, 30, 34–5
Declaration of the Rights of Man 22, 23, 24
democratic freedoms 23
Directory 42, 44

Enlightenment 10, 25
Estates-General 8, 10, 12, 27

First Estate 8, 14, 16, 24
food supplies 21, 42
foreign invasion, threat of 26, 28, 34
French revolutionary wars 28, 30

Glorious Revolution (Britain) 4
government, system of 4, 8
guillotine 4, 32, 33, 36, 37

Hugo, Victor 48, 49

'La Marseillaise' 29
Lafayette, Marquis de 20, 38
Legislative Assembly 28, 30
'Liberty, Equality, Fraternity' 22, 48, 50
Louis XVI 4, 5, 8, 10, 14, 16, 17, 20, 26, 27, 30, 32–3, 34, 50

Marie Antoinette 7, 8, 9, 38
Mirabeau, Comte de 12

Napoleon Bonaparte 44–7, 50
National Assembly/National Constituent Assembly 5, 12, 14, 16, 20, 22, 24, 25, 26
National Convention 30, 32, 34, 36, 40, 41, 42
National Guard 20
Necker, Jacques 16, 18, 20
nobles 8, 12, 14, 24, 25, 28

Palais-Royal gardens 12, 13
primary and secondary sources of information 6–7
propaganda 7

radicalism 5, 10, 20, 24, 30, 32, 36, 42, 46, 49
Reign of Terror 38, 40, 41, 50
republicans 26, 28, 32, 39, 49
riots 18, 20, 21
Robespierre, Maximilien 38, 39, 40, 41
royalists 34, 39

Second Estate 8, 14, 16, 24
'September massacres' 7, 30, 31
Sieyès, Emmanuel-Joseph 15, 22

taxation 4, 8, 9, 10, 11, 14
Tennis Court Oath 14, 15
Third Estate 8, 10, 11, 12, 14, 15, 16, 17, 18, 27, 50
Tocqueville, Alexis de 50, 51
Trafalgar, Battle of 46
tribunals 36, 38
Tuileries, storming of the 30

universal suffrage 32

Versailles 10, 16
voting rights 10, 12, 32